The Invisible Woman: From Combat to Wholeness

A Combat Veteran Struggles to Find Her Place in a Chaotic World

Katina L. Patterson
with Tracey Nicole Hayes, Ph.D.

The Invisible Woman:
From Combat to Wholeness

A combat veteran struggles to find her place in a chaotic world

Katina L. Patterson
with Tracey Nicole Hayes, Ph.D.

The Invisible Woman: From Combat to Wholeness
Copyright © 2020 by Katina L. Patterson. All rights reserved.

This work contains adult language and is intended for readers above the age of 18.

No part of this publication may be reproduced, stored in a retrieval system, or transmitted in any way, by any means whether electronically, mechanically, via photocopy, recording, or otherwise without the prior written permission of the publisher except as provided by US copyright law.

Scripture quotations marked KJV are from the King James version of the *Holy Bible*. Public Domain.

Scripture quotations marked MSG are taken from *THE MESSAGE (MSG)*, copyright © 1993, 2002, 2018 by Eugene H. Peterson. Used by permission of NavPress. All rights reserved. Represented by Tyndale House Publishers, Inc.

Published in the United States by Katina L. Patterson

Publishing assistance, cover design and interior layout provided by TJS Publishing House, www.tjspublishinghouse.com

Editing by Tracey Nicole Hayes, Ph.D.
www.jhwritingplus.com

Paperback ISBN-13: 978-0-578-64064-8
Paperback ISBN-10: 0-578-64064-3

To "Joe"

Contents

Introduction	i
Chapter 1: The Beginning	1
Chapter 2: Civilian to Soldier	7
Chapter 3: Life in War	21
Chapter 4: Unbearable Pain	39
Chapter 5: Finding My Way	51
Chapter 6: God's Hand Directing My Steps	61
Chapter 7: Recognizing My Weakness	67
Chapter 8: Loving Ourselves	75
Chapter 9: Purpose, Plan and Process to Wholeness	79

Introduction

I never had it in my mind to write this book. First of all, I am *not* a writer. Secondly, I didn't really want people to come into my world. I have always desired to live a simple life; however, God said otherwise. I was asleep one night, and God awoke me and said, "You have to tell your story." Let me tell you why.

Life is full of mysteries. There are many mysteries in this life which are far beyond our imaginations. It's common for us to want our lives to be very easy with no problems. Most of us want the big house, the white picket fence, the two children. We want to live very well without challenge, without obstacle, without stress or strain. Some may want to be rich and travel the world, while others may just want their little piece of paradise in the stillness of their own backyards. Well, that's not always the case. Life can throw us for a loop in a moment's notice and at every chance possible. The question is, how are we going to handle those challenges? Are we going to throw in the towel? Are we going to lie in our beds and hide from the world and wish life away? Or are we going to face life head on? Those are some of the questions we must ask ourselves when life throws everything it has at us.

When I retired from the Army, God spoke to me and asked me to return to my hometown of Madison, North Carolina. He said these exact words: "The kids are dying and have no hope." Hearing this made my head, heart, and every part of my being hurt. Just the enormity of it all coupled with the fact that I had no plans on returning to North Carolina, *period!*

I remember informing my mother when I left home at the age of eighteen that I would be back to visit, but never to live. *How funny is that?* After God spoke to me, I prayed, cried, and like the biblical Jonah even tried to run from moving to Madison, North Carolina, but I couldn't get out of it. On March 1, 2013, I relocated back home.

Now, as God usually does to me, He gave me one simple directive. I was to come home to give speeches encouraging young kids to follow their dreams and to push them to their next levels. My task was to make them see that it was okay to take that leap of faith. The message I was to give to them was simple: You can pursue higher education. You can do big things. Whatever your dreams are, you can achieve them. If you can dream it, you can be it.

The message was simple enough, but all the while, I was asking God, "what about *me*?" I needed to be healed and made whole, and I was far from that point when God spoke. I was coming out of my combat boots and into a world I knew nothing about. My entire adult life had been service to others, to my country. But what about *me*? In making the transition, I felt and sometimes still feel like an invisible woman in a world of civilians who didn't know how to tell time, how to talk, how to walk, or how to think! *Or was that me?* How would I make it in this world? How would I help *myself*? All of these things were going through my head. This book, *The Invisible Woman: From Combat to Wholeness* was born out of these questions.

Chapter 1

The Beginning

I grew up as a little girl in the small town of Madison, North Carolina. The population was roughly about 2,100 people. I grew up in what I would consider an average family: Mom, Dad, five sisters and me. When discussing my upbringing, some of my friends would say, "You had a lot more than the average child." Well, I didn't see it that way. True, my family lived in a house, and most of my friends lived in trailers. Most of my friends got reduced lunch, and I didn't. Most of them were from single parent households, and I had both my parents. So socioeconomically, I may have had more, but I saw all of us as being equal. I was just a kid trying to fit in with everyone else. To me, we were all normal, average kids.

My mother was very strict, which I suppose is to be expected with six girls. I had a curfew and it felt like I couldn't go anywhere. My friends didn't even bother asking me if I could go places because the answer would be 'no.'

There was a significant age difference between my three older sisters and myself, and when they moved out, I was left to help with my younger twin sisters. Those were some of the hardest years of my young life. I was about fourteen years old then, and the twins were just four. In my mind, I wondered how I was supposed to cope with two identical twins that were into everything? And for ten years, I had been the baby of the family. Now I felt overwhelmed with responsibility. Being from a close-knit family like mine, however, with a *very old school* mom who belonged to the "do as I say, and not as I do" school of thought, I learned to comply.

I helped take care of my younger sisters throughout my high school years while my parents worked. Sometimes I felt trapped with the level of responsibility I had. Everywhere I went if I went anywhere the twins went. I was going to school, playing basketball and softball, working, watching the twins, and still managed to maintain a 3.5 GPA in high school. With all of my hard work and dedication, I thought I would be set for college after I graduated.

I desperately wanted to get away, and I was applying to schools all over the state. It was my senior year, and I had taken the SAT. I was more than ready to go. I was accepted into Fayetteville State University and just the thought of being two hours away from Madison was so exciting. To my shock and surprise, my mom strongly disagreed with my plans to leave home, even though we had had this discussion before about me going to college.

"No!" she said. "Absolutely not. You can attend the community college, get a job, and help pay for your education because we do *not* have that type of money to send you to a four-year college!"

I was heartbroken! I had worked so hard. I couldn't go to the college I desperately wanted to attend.

"God, why?"

That was the only question I could scream and cry. *"Why?"* After all that I had gone through to get to this point. *What next? How am I going to make my dreams of leaving this small town a reality?* I had no other plans. I was a 17-year-old high school student who worked part-time at the Winn-Dixie grocery store. How could I afford to pay for college? How could I manifest any of my plans? All of those questions went through my head and I just cried. That curveball life threw at me hit hard.

Just a few days after my dreams of attending college were shattered, I was walking in my school when I noticed an Army recruiter. I had never had any prior thoughts of joining the Army at all. I remember I once hung up on a recruiter when they called my house to speak to me. (I was nasty to them that day. God has a way of humbling us.) I had nothing to lose, so I stopped and talked to him. He gave me information on how the Army could give me a career and pay for my college education altogether. *Wow!* If the Army could do that for me, then joining the Army would be my new plan.

I ran home and informed my mother about how I could pay for college by joining the Army. *Bam!* She stopped me dead in my tracks.

"You are *not* joining the Army!" she said.

No explanation was given, but I knew a lot of it had to do with my responsibilities with caring for my now elementary-aged twin sisters. I was in disbelief. It was going to cost her nothing, it was all on me. I felt hurt all over again. I was screaming inside and asking God *"why?"* again. *"Why does it seem like you are not allowing me to leave Madison, North Carolina?"*

I was only seventeen years old then, and I needed my mother's permission to join the Army. The legal age to join the Army without permission is eighteen, so without her permission, I couldn't join.

Back when I was growing up, kids didn't question or second-guess their parents, but that day I was bold. I mustered up enough nerve to inform my mother that I *was* going to join the Army when I turned eighteen, and that I *was* leaving Madison. (Now mind you, I did this out of her arms reach so she wouldn't slap the taste out of my mouth!) She saw the determination in my eyes. We set a date for the Army Recruiter to come over and speak with my mother to give her the ins and outs of the Army. I was still unsure which direction it would go. *Guess what?* She signed! I was now a U.S. Army Private!

Chapter 2

Civilian to Soldier

The country girl from Madison was now in the U.S. Army. I soon discovered that enlisting in the Army is not anything like the movies. I was now in Fort Jackson, South Carolina, three-and-a-half hours away from everything I knew. I was no longer Katina; I was Private Patterson and every other name under the sun. I found out the phrase "hurry up and wait" was a true statement. We literally ran to everything only to stand in line and wait. My mind questioned a lot of things I observed. *Why do we run so*

much? Why am I just a number? Did I make the right decision?

From the day I got off the bus at Fort Jackson for Army Basic Training, I belonged to the United States Government. Now some may ask, why in the world would anyone choose a life like this? Contrary to popular belief, regimented life was not and is not all bad. Yes, we had rules to abide by, and we had people to answer to. But don't we have that on every job? Through my inward questioning and observations, I soon learned the Army had a method and reason for everything that was taught.

The Army provided me with adult structure. My mother was strict, but her kind of structure didn't allow for any autonomy on my part. Army structure taught me how to communicate and speak up for myself. I knew what time I was waking up every morning, what time I was saluting the flag, and what time was allotted for physical training. I knew what time was given for meals and almost what time I could use the *latrine* (another name for the restroom). All through that training period, I was learning how to become a Soldier. I was learning basic skillsets of life, and guess what? I was getting paid every 1st and 15th of the month. Not to mention, I was receiving money to fulfill my dream of going to college.

Coming from a small town, I was now exposed to diversities I had never known before. I was taught how to get along with others, a skill many people would benefit from learning today. I found out that we may not have liked our "Battle Buddies," but we had better get along in the eyes of the Drill Sergeants! A *Battle Buddy* was an assigned peer, and it was mandated for us to be together constantly wherever we went. If we got caught without our buddy, there would be *hell* to pay. That was not the punishment anyone wanted.

We had to make sure we learned everything about our buddy their parents, family members, hopes and dreams because we couldn't go anywhere without them. As for my buddy, I felt we were protection for one another, and there was a safety in being with her.

Lights-out in Basic Training was at 2100hrs (9 p.m.) nightly, but I wondered, *if we go to bed so early, how are we supposed to get everything accomplished for the next day?* That's where our time management skills were put to the test. I had to ask myself, do I want to sleep, or do I want to study to pass this test tomorrow? We learned to prioritize and make decisions based on what activity we considered most important.

The job of the drill instructors was to transform us from civilian to Soldier by teaching us the Army values: Loyalty, Duty, Respect, Selfless Service, Honor, Integrity, and Personal Courage. I slowly began my transformation into a United States Army Soldier.

Honestly, I had already learned most of those values from my mother. She taught me that if I was going to do something, *do my best.* I had the mindset that I was going to be the best Private Patterson there was. Nothing less was for me.

When I entered Army Basic Training, the country was already at war in Operation Desert Shield. American troops were part of an international coalition in the war against Iraq, including a tremendous increase in U.S. forces to the Persian Gulf. What did that mean for my training class? To my fellow female Soldiers and me, this meant nothing. There were restrictions against women serving in combat ground positions. Like the other women, I knew I'd probably have a desk job when my training was complete.

But the Army was known for training hard even when the country was not at war. The instructors drilled it into our heads that we were training to go to war *all* of us. They weren't training administrative personnel; they were training fighters. Warriors. We were not yet done with our training, but honestly, I was praying that the war would be over before our training was finished.

Finally, graduation from Army Basic Training was upon us, and I was going to see my family. It was a beautiful sight. I was so glad to see everybody, especially my mom. Likewise, she was glad to see what a big difference U.S. Army Basic Training had made in me. I saw my family only for a few short hours, but that meant the world to me. Sadly, some Soldiers didn't have any family members come to see them transition from a wide-eyed civilian to a true Soldier. I never took for granted the sacrifice my family made to come see me graduate.

The next phase in our training was the specialty phase known as Advanced Individual Training, or AIT. The friends we made in Army Basic Training who didn't have the same specialty left and went elsewhere to continue their training. The hardest part of military life is the "see you later."

We never say goodbye in the military. No matter how big you think it is, the military is really small and we were sure to run into the same people again later. I stayed at Fort Jackson to complete my specialty training. The war effort escalated daily it seemed but I knew I wasn't going into anything too "hardcore." I was designated as an Administrative Specialist and that was going to land me an office job. It was a safe posting, and I was pretty much assured I would not see any combat, primarily because that was the law.

I remember being so happy to join the Army, knowing I was going to get my choice of career field as an Administrative Specialist. That job was going to open up so many opportunities, even after a full career in the military. I was thinking long-term with this career. (I remember my recruiter till this day. He was great.)

Our time at AIT was drawing to a close. I was excitedly preparing to go to my office job. Even though there was a new fight for women to be able to go to war and engage in direct combat, I didn't really want a "dirty" job. Given the choice between being a mechanic, and handling pay disbursement, I readily chose the latter. Regardless of the law, I also knew I didn't want the mental anguish I could only imagine front line experience would bring.

It was almost time to graduate from AIT. On the night before we were to see our families, about thirty-five of us were informed to meet in the dayroom of our barracks at 1800hrs (6 p.m.). We were all laughing and joking, giving high-fives all around because we were going to become full-fledged U.S. Army Soldiers the next day.

All the Drill Sergeants (non commis-sioned officers) came in laughing and joking. They didn't know the reason for the impromptu meeting either; they thought we were in trouble and the First Sergeant (senior non-commissioned officer) was getting ready to lay it on us one last time. However, that was not the case.

The First Sergeant entered the room, and we silenced ourselves without a command. He always looked serious and displeased, but this time his demeanor was different. He started by stating that the country was at full-blown ground war. The buildup of troops for Desert Shield had morphed into the combat phase of Desert Storm, and we the Soldiers had direct orders to support the war.

"For everyone that's in this room," he began, "you're on individual orders to the Middle East in support of Operation Desert Storm."

His eyes looked like he had seen a ghost. There was pin-drop silence.

At that moment, I felt all the air go straight out of my body. I couldn't breathe, talk or move. I think one Soldier screamed and everyone including me ran to contact our family members. That is the only thing I remember about that moment.

By the time I made it to the stairwell leading up to our barracks, I passed out. I was in shock. I knew in the back of my mind that combat deployment was a possibility, but I always thought if it did happen, it would be after I had gotten to my unit and integrated. By then, I would know who I could trust and those whom I might have to keep a good eye on. All during training, we had our buddy's back. Now I wouldn't have a buddy to have my back, or me to have theirs. I wouldn't know anyone, a Private straight out of training. I was mentally exhausted and I hadn't even left.

I don't know how long I was out, but when I finally came to, I ran straight to the community phone. There was a long line of people waiting to call home. Panic. Crying. Sheer disbelief. The ones that weren't being deployed were either in stark silence or consoling us with insufficient words of comfort. I imagined my family's faces, and what their responses might be. I was at a complete loss. When it was my turn to call home, my mom had barely answered when I screamed, "Don't come!! Don't come, I'm going to war!"

My mom was silent on the other end. When she finally spoke, she said: "We are still coming."

I kept on screaming. "No! Don't come!"

The thought of seeing them for what could be my last time was too much for me to bear, and I didn't want my mom to go through that pain either. I wasn't prepared, and I wanted to just say "see you later" over the phone because I didn't know if I would actually see them later.

Well, that didn't work as my mom could not be dissuaded. The next morning when it was time to meet up with my family, I had more family members than I could have ever imagined. My step-dad had a van and it was full of my family coming to see me graduate and become a United States Army Soldier. That was one of the proudest and saddest moments of my life. About fourteen people piled out of that van that day.

When I put my uniform on that morning, I felt confident. *We've trained for this. I'm going to be okay*, I thought.

As I stood for graduation, I reminisced on the fact that a couple of my classmates hadn't made it to that day. I had set my mind to graduate, and passed everything the first time. I got my ribbon and I was a bona fide Soldier. At the same time, I was a bona fide Soldier and I couldn't go home. My service was to start immediately. I saw the worry behind the smiles of my family, the pride mixed with sadness in their eyes.

That was over twenty-eight years ago, and the pain, the panic, the anxiety, the memories are still vivid today. Watching the news today, my palms get sweaty and I just cry for my brothers and sisters I see going to war, knowing the imminent danger they will face in defense of this great nation. I love to see reunification videos, I feel so elated and bask in the glow, but that is short-lived because I know what's to come with the night sweats and terrors of war visiting in the middle of the day after the things they've seen.

At the end of the ceremony, we only had a few hours to eat and say our farewells. Normally, I would have been able to go home for a week or two, but we didn't even get to spend the night with our families because we were on orders to war. What had once been fear was replaced with disbelief and quickly turned to mild defiance toward our senior leadership in the form of drinking and staying up past lights-out. It wasn't anyone's fault, but the thought was among many: "What else could they do to us?" We were locked down on post, preventing the possibility of AWOL (Absent Without Leave). My bags were packed and we were going to move to the mobilization site at Ft. Jackson the day after graduation. I hugged everyone and told them not to cry, that I would see them later. They cried anyway.

I held it together until I saw my family's van fade away over the hill out of sight. Then I fell apart. Every piece of energy I had holding me together drained from my body. I had nothing more. My Battle Buddy, the same one from bootcamp, was right by my side. I collapsed to the ground. She picked me up.

"You're going to be okay," she said. "Get up. Let's go."

I dusted it off, as we like to say. *I'm a Soldier*, I reminded myself, *suck it up and move on.*

My Battle Buddy wasn't one of the thirty-five of us going to war; she was going to her original duty station. Both of us had been raised in the church. She kept telling me God had a plan and a purpose, and everything was going to be alright.

She had been with me from our initial Army training and she knew what was happening. She was there to literally pick me up when I felt down. She was there to encourage me and help me think positively. When life throws a curveball, we really need someone who is going to be a positive reinforcement for us when everything looks like doom and gloom. We need someone who can tell us when we feel like we can't go on, "Oh, yes, you can!" For me, this situation was the epitome of doom and gloom, and she was right by my side.

Chapter 3

Life in War

Who would have ever thought that at the tender age of eighteen I would be off in a faraway land fight-ing a war? Not me! I had other plans for my life. I was a country girl with my eyes set on going to college, but here came life's curveball. *How was I going to handle it?*

I grew up in church and knew how to pray. I knew God was my protector. I knew my mother, family, church, and friends were praying for my safety. Yet, I was mad. All my anger was squarely directed at God. *Why did my life have to be like this? I questioned. Why couldn't I go to college and enjoy the college life I planned?* Now, I was off to go and fight in a war. *Perhaps God doesn't love me anymore,* I thought to myself, and I resigned myself to that thought. Many people have had the same thoughts about God not loving them anymore. (Honestly, have you had such a thought before?)

The tension was thick and surreal on the 16-hour flight. It was early February 1991, and I remember being half asleep on the flight to Kuwait, a tiny Arab country sitting on the northern end of the Persian Gulf, holding Saudi Arabia and Iraq as its border nations. I woke just as we were getting into Kuwaiti airspace. When I saw the fighter jets that were to escort us to the runway, I lost it. I screamed. I cried. I assumed the pilot had flown into enemy territory and the fighter jets were enemy planes that had intercepted us. One of my best friends was on the plane with me, seated just in front of me. We grabbed one another thinking we were under attack, just two 18-year-old kids not knowing anything that was going on. The older Soldier beside me reassured me that the jets were just guiding us to a safe landing. *Whew!* I was so relieved to hear that. We landed safely in Kuwait (KKMC), the replacement detachment, a series of buildings just miles from the Iraqi border. My friend and I were both designated as personnel (71L), so we were requested by rate. But we were all trained as Soldiers an allegiance to our country, not a rate.

I didn't feel as though I truly knew my job; I had book knowledge the regulatory guidance but you learn your job by doing your job. I couldn't fathom the reality that I was sent to a war-zone to type a memorandum! It felt like an oxymoron.

"First to Fire, First to Fall," was a saying we had. Regardless of my rate, I was first a Soldier, and if I had to, I would have to fire first, or I would fall first. If I had to lay ground fire, lock and load, kill someone, that's what I would have to do because I was determined to make it out of the war alive.

I remember standing alongside my friend at a table where we received our assignments. We kept asking if we could stay together, and were told repeatedly "no." We had made up in our minds that they were going to take us together. We locked our weapons around each other, mine around her and hers around me.

"You can make room for one more personnel soldier!" we demanded.

Senior personnel tried pulling us apart, but we refused. Finally, someone unhooked us and we found ourselves separated, crying, begging, to no avail.

Scud missile warnings went off at random, routine intervals. I slept with my gas mask next to me on the hard floor in a sleeping bag of a makeshift barracks. These tactical ballistic missiles landed all around me, though Patriot missile interceptors prevented them from actually hitting my building, breaking many of them up in the sky. Sirens blared in the distance. I couldn't tell if it was real, imagined, or how close the missiles were coming. It was constant. I would awake in the middle of the night to alarms, and I was defiant with anger and fear. I made up in mind I would only put my gas mask on if and when a missile landed near me. It was 110 degrees in the desert and the gas mask was suffocating. I decided to take my chances.

My stay at that particular location was only temporary, and then I left to go meet my unit in the desert. Two days later, the missile interceptor failed, and the building I had once slept in for about a week was hit with a scud missile.

I was fortunate enough to be posted to a National Guard unit from Henderson, North Carolina, about two hours away from my hometown. This made me feel like I had some people from home there with me who would look out for me. I was young, but my unit had a lot of older women that had been down this road before in the military, though none of them had been to war. I knew how to function based on regulation, but I had never done anything like this before. They were supportive, and they knew I was young and helped me.

I felt a little relieved to be with this unit, but I was still mad with God. I'm not going to sugarcoat it writing this book is a part of my healing from combat to my journey towards wholeness. In my plan, I had wanted to go to college and since I had to find another route, I chose the military. Going into the military was never supposed to be my life, and certainly not going to war. I felt things should have turned out differently. Honestly, I was more scared than mad, but mad was my default emotion.

When I arrived at 30th Support Group (a personnel unit) and met those in charge, my Operations Officer an Army Major told me, "Private Patterson, once this war ends, I will put you on the first flight back home." I asked him to promise me that he'd do as he said, and he promised. But he, nor anyone else, had any idea when the war would end. Still, I had hope.

I was given my work area and the tent where I was to sleep in the desert. Like everyone else, I was issued a total of forty live rounds. *First to fire, first to fall.* I was prepared to protect myself. Afterward, I got to meet other people in the unit. I began to think that things were not as bad as I thought they would be. However, I always reminded myself that it was war and in war, anything could happen.

On the first night of my arrival, I asked if I could go to the nearest phone station a telecommunications unit on another compound in the desert to call my mother and inform her I had arrived safely in Kuwait. One of the other Soldiers planned to call his family that night when there wouldn't be a long line. He said he knew how to get to the phones at the telecommunications hub, and he promised to take me along. We made it to the telecommunications unit without incident; however, on the way back, I knew something wasn't right. We were definitely off base. When I saw grass and brown desert kangaroos hopping, I knew we were wrong. We were based in the desert, so grass and kangaroo weren't remotely what we were supposed to see.

"Where the hell are we? Are we in another country?" I said, clutching my weapon, ready to lock and load.

I had never "locked and loaded" with a live round without being told. I went into panic mode, but at the same time I was prepared for war. *First to fire, first to fall.* Instinct kicked in.

I prayed. *Lord, please help us. I am not going to die like this. This is not how this chapter of my life is going to end 'Soldier Dies Trying to Find Telephone Station in the Desert!'*

We were lost for over two hours. I had learned map reading in training before, but everything was flat, empty desert and I had no point of reference. There was no light, and there was "mandatory blackout driving" covers placed on our headlights to prevent enemy detection. We came upon another unit in the desert, and they had radio telecommunication. The other Soldier knew the radio line to our unit, and someone was always monitoring the line. He gave them our grid coordinates.

I sat in the truck with tears rolling down my face, screaming with no one to hear, "I'm not going to die in this desert trying to make a phone call!"

He had gotten the coordinates to where we were and navigated back to the base. My trust level was down and my pulse was racing. We used our compass to get back to base in complete darkness. From that point on, I never went to the telephone stations with him, and I never went unless it was daylight. It was so easy to get turned around and lost in the desert. Eventually, engineers ended up building mile markers so we knew where we were, but at the time I arrived, there was only miles and miles and miles of desert land.

All along, God was showing me he had me covered, but I was still mad at him. I questioned why he let me be drafted into the war and why he didn't cause my life to turn out differently?

That first night with my new unit, I was miserable. It was even worse than sleeping on the floor in a sleeping bag. I had a cot with my sleeping bag rolled out, no mattress, and about 15 women in one tent with no showers. Fifteen women; no showers. *How did we bathe?* We took showers out of our Kevlar helmets, flipping the helmet upside down, filling the helmet with water, and washing down that way for about a week until the engineers came and built "showers." Two shower stalls were built one male, one female. We would pull a lever, wet ourselves down, turn the lever off, soap up, and pull the lever back on to rinse. Shower done. If anyone had even thought about keeping the water running through that thin pipe to enjoy a tiny luxury, they would have incurred the wrath of the entire unit for their indulgence. There was a shortage of water in the middle of the desert and we used generator power to run showers and provide lighting. But my first night there, and after being lost in the desert for two hours, the last thing I was thinking about was shower facilities.

There was nothing around us but concertina wire, or what we called "Constantine wire" large, coiled barbed wire with spikes and that was our protection. Men and women were on security watch, roaming the compound. Never say it can't get any worse. At least at KKMC, I was in a building.

Fighter planes were constantly flying overhead. I knew by default that I was on the "friendly" side, but I also was aware of "friendly fire." After being lost in the desert just a few hours earlier with everything looking the same, how could I be certain these fighter pilots wouldn't find themselves in a similar situation turned around and disoriented and accidentally drop a bomb on my location? I was on high-alert with fear, thinking of the possibility one of the U.S. planes might accidentally drop a bomb on us.

Kuwaiti Bedouins roamed the land their land herding sheep, but we didn't know if they were coming up to our campgrounds out of curiosity or with bombs. They came so close to the campgrounds until they were instructed to move. We couldn't be too trusting in times of war. I imagine they were intrigued with our large military presence where nothing had been before for as far as the eye could see. No mile markers, no trees. Just desert.

All was quiet on the home front (as we used to say in the Army) as the days went by, until one night in February. We had a meeting to inform us of the NATO coalition multinational infantry brigades crossing over into Iraq in search of Sadam Hussein to put an end to the war. We were told to be on high alert and be ready to receive causalities during the ground war. There was a possibility we would experience food and water shortage as everything was being pushed to support the Soldiers on the front line. My heart sunk. I was just an eighteen-year-old country girl in a far-away land. I started thinking about a lot of things. *Did I say the right thing to my family? What did I do or what didn't I do? Did I tell my Mom I loved her? Did I tell my sisters to be good in school? Did I do this, did I do that?* The thoughts were endless. If I didn't make it back home, would someone be there to help my family? How, what, when, where, and why?

We made a "run" to the exchange and bought bottled water and noodles in case we ran out of food. Trades were made. The anxiety was nerve-racking. We were preparing for the worst.

That night I stood outside my tent and watched the bombs fall, one after another. My tent shook, the sky went red, and my tears were falling. I was standing there, seeing it all with my own eyes. *Lord, keep me, help me*, I prayed earnestly. *I know I am a fool and I have done foolish things, but this is real. If I am to make it home, it is by your grace and mercy.*

While I was at war, I saw things that still keep me awake at night. No matter how I try to block it out, I still see these things. Unbelievable is an understatement. The sky was lit in reds and blues. The smell of bombs is something I can't describe. My mind raced, knowing bombs were hitting people, children, homes, schools. I could look up and see planes refueling overhead to bomb more. The ground shook. I wanted to scream and cry. *This is not happening right before my eyes,* I told myself in ineffective hopes of consolation.

I rationalized.

I commanded myself to pray.

I entertained conflicting emotions. The people of the country didn't deserve what their leader was doing. Still, they stood by him. I hated the bombs dropping, but told myself, *it's not me dropping the bombs.* But by virtue of me having joined the Army, I supported the bombs being dropped.

Nevertheless, the war was over quickly. It ended early April of 1991, and true to the Major's word, I was sent back to U.S. soil. I threw everything all my clothes, everything into a burn pile. I turned my suitcase upside down to make sure there wasn't a grain of sand in my bags. I gave away everything else. I heard people were being turned back for having contraband sand, Iraqi AK47s, all kinds of souvenirs from the war. I didn't want to carry anything back I didn't go over with. I had my sleeping bag and my weapon, only the required gear I had to turn in with me.

When I got on the plane and settled down, the tears flowed at the knowledge I was going home. When the pilot said, "We have left Saudi/Kuwaiti international air space," the plane erupted in cheers. I laid my seat back and slept most of the way. Finally, I got my first rest.

I was home for my mother's birthday on April 17, 1991. I believe that my coming home was one of the best birthday presents she has had. For me, it was an opportunity to see the smile on her face. I had the opportunity of not just seeing my mom but my entire family. My sisters showed me a collection of all the newspapers my mother had saved while I was at war, telling me the news stayed on the television constantly.

Now that I'd made it back, how was I to start my healing process? How was I to heal myself of the brokenness of what I'd gone through? Back then, there was a minimal debriefing process after returning from war. Like everyone else, I went through "demobing" or demobilizing the process of making sure I returned all of my issued gear, and that my physical health was satisfactory before being sent to my next duty station. This procedure did nothing to assist with mental health. My generation was never able to discuss what had happened. We were Soldiers first, trained to fight, trained to kill. We were never able to talk about the hurt and pain and grief. I rationalized to myself and to anyone who cared to listen that I could do everything I was big and bad enough to do; I was a war veteran. What could anyone do to me that I hadn't been through already?

There was an unwritten, widely accepted rule: No one talked about the mental effects of the war. No one shared if they were suffering. Since no one talked about it, no one knew if anyone else was feeling the same effects they were. In this area, there was a fundamental lack of trust no one could be confided in. If anyone sought after mental health, it was a career-ender. The stigma was awful. I was assigned to a new unit. I picked up and shipped out.

I was stationed in Fort Jackson, South Carolina for eight months. I partied to mask the pain. "Oh, you're a Soldier suck it up and move on," was the general attitude. So, that was exactly what I did I sucked it up and moved on to my next assignment in Frankfurt, Germany for two years. I extended my enlistment overseas so that when I wanted to get out of the military, I would be in the states and better able to transition to civilian life or so I thought. I moved to Alexandria, Virginia for a year. My total first enlistment was four year and nine months.

I left the Army because I was tired of saying farewell to my friends. I had no plan, no direction, I just repeatedly said goodbye to friends that became family. This time, I was saying goodbye to the Army.

I moved back home for six months, and thought, "North Carolina is not it." Civilian life did not fit for me. I thought, maybe it's Madison, North Carolina that doesn't fit for me. So, I moved to Maryland to an apartment that still had the chalk outline of a body when I moved in. I ate Oodles of Noodles at ten cents a box. I stayed out for only one year before I realized, the Army was where I was to be. I had a heart to heart with my favorite uncle, and I gained a lot of clarity.

"Say, say? What's your plan?" he said to me.

I had almost five years of enlisted service with what I felt was nothing to show for it. I had gained weight. I was in poor physical and mental health. I had nothing to show for all that I had experienced.

"You're going to go back in and retire from the military," my uncle said. "When you think your Plan A isn't working, what's your Plan B? When your Plan B isn't working, you go back to Plan A!"

My Plan A was the U.S. Army, so I reenlisted. If it wasn't for my uncle, I can only wonder where I would be today.

Chapter 4

Unbearable Pain

Throughout my Army career I had many assignments. After I re-enlisted in the Army, I was stationed in San Antonio, Texas. I was at my seventeen year po-int. A couple of new Soldiers arrived at the same time, too. One of the Soldiers, Sergeant First Class "Joe" and I became great friends; he had been enlisted for eighteen, going on nineteen, years. He had many deployments to the Middle East as a military intelligence soldier that he couldn't really talk about, but we talked about everything else under the sun. Joe had a name for me that only he could say he called me "Patty Cake."

I loved the friendship Joe and I shared. He had blond hair, blue eyes, an infectious smile, and was quick to blush. One day he got a sharp haircut, and I commented on how nice it looked.

"Go ahead," he said, as he bent his head toward me, "I know you wanna touch this haircut!"

I ruffled his hair back and forth, and we just laughed. It became a greeting ritual with us. He would walk in and without a word, he would bend his head toward me. I would tousle his hair and we would laugh uncontrollably. That's how we would start our workday together.

Joe smiled and smiled and smiled.

Sometimes Joe would look at me and smile so wide, but the pain in his eyes was so visible. Without him ever having to say a word to me, I would just say, "Every day is a new day, Joe, a new opportunity." I knew behind his smile was a terrible hurt.

As senior ranking non-commissioned officers, we're held to a higher standard, presumably able to shake anything off, salute the flag and move it out. Sometimes, we look good on paper, as if we are superheroes. And sometimes, it's all we can do to just get up in the morning after a fitful, sweat-soaked night of fighting demons from wars many have long since forgotten, if they ever knew at all.

We were a teaching unit. We taught Military Intelligence and prepared units to deploy, but when having anxiety, he wasn't always able to can't teach effectively. Plus, Joe was naturally an introvert anyway, and preferred to be behind the scenes. I noticed Joe was suffering from severe Post Traumatic Stress Disorder (PTSD). He got up to teach and he stuttered. Sometimes, Joe would literally be shaking with anxiety whenever he had to be in front of people, which was the continual nature of the job. His anxiety grew increasingly worse, and our peers were less than empathetic. He confided in me that he was suffering. I had compassion for his condition brought about by the unimaginable images that haunted him, but other people didn't always understand.

We had a long talk one day and he said, "Patty Cake, I need help." I knew from the tone of his voice that he was very serious and could no longer hide his pain. He was sliding fast on a downward slope. I knew I had to jump into action to get my friend help. He was not going to be a part of the 22 Soldiers who committed suicide daily. Not on my watch.

Even though we were the same rank, I advocated on his behalf and asked that Joe be detailed to me. There was a new realization by military leadership and health professionals that people needed mental health assistance without jeopardizing their security clearances, and there was a need to erase the stigmas associated with the emotional consequences of war. I was able to get him into a military program that helped Soldiers with PTSD and other related issues. He enjoyed the program and we chatted almost every day about his improvements, upcoming retirement, and pretty much everything. We were very close friends and grew even closer. Going to PTSD class helped him significantly, and he was excited to know he wasn't alone in his condition. He completed the program, came back to the unit and worked in my office. I wanted him to stay where he was, but my request was denied. We laughed, joked, and enjoyed our time together. I prayed with him often and told him he was going to be just fine. I told him, "Get a dog. If you get a dog, you're going to meet a woman. Women love dogs." He took my advice, got a dog, and met his girlfriend. "The pooch got you a dog!" I said, jokingly.

"Patty Cake," he said, "thank you for caring about me and being a friend."

"You're more than welcome," I said. "We are Soldiers, and you know what that means? We are family."

Later in the year, I received orders to relocate to Fort Knox, Kentucky. Immediately, I went through my "God, why?" questions again. I felt at home in San Antonio. I loved my church, my home, and I loved my unit. Everything was going great. Why would I have to relocate? *Why now?* Change can be so hard. There goes that curveball!

I knew I had to tell Joe that it was time for me to go. I was going to miss his big heart when I left. When I informed him, I could see the disappointment in his eyes. He was devastated.

"Why do you have to go?" he asked. "Can't you decline the assignment?"

I couldn't. I had been nominated for the assignment to work in the General Officer

Management Office, and although I felt the timing was all wrong, it was the professional opportunity of a lifetime.

"I know I'm being selfish," Joe said, "but you are truly a good friend."

I sighed and shrugged and shook my head. "I've been selected," I said. "I can't turn down the GOMO."

"You're the only person that cares about me, Patty Cake," he said.

"Joe, you're doing great," I said. "I'm so proud of you. Just one more year and you'll retire. You'll be just fine. If there's anyone I will get on a plane to come back to see, it will be you."

"I'm not coming to your farewell party," Joe said. "You know I can't say goodbye to you."

"We don't say 'bye,' Joe," I reminded him. "We say, 'see you later!'"

We talked for a while as we always did. I pinky-promised that we would both be okay, and he gave me his signature big grin. When it was my final day at the unit, I was hopeful, but I knew my

Soldier buddy would not be there. He couldn't stand even the thought of saying goodbye.

Before I left, I asked the First Sergeant to keep an eye on my friend because I wasn't sure he was really okay. All of the signs were there to label Joe as a suicide risk, but he hadn't outright said he was suicidal. The command did collect Joe's guns but had to give them back because they had no legal reason to keep them. Ideally, there would have been a command referral that would then have gone to the local sheriff to mandate keeping the guns, but the guns were given back.

I made it to Fort Knox, and I had settled in for about thirty days when I received the call. I heard an internal voice say to me twice "Don't go home," so I went to the Horseshoe casino. On a clear afternoon on April 16, 2001, my phone rang.

"Hello?"

"Sergeant First Class Patterson, where are you?"

I recognized the number but not the voice, and said, "I'm in Fort Knox, what's wrong?"

"We have something to tell you," the voice on the other end continued. "It's Joe."

"No. No, no, no, no, no."

"Your Soldier friend here in San Antonio committed suicide last night."

I fell to the floor and screamed at the top of my lungs. I had no feelings. I had just gotten to Fort Knox. Nobody knew me. Would anyone care that another Soldier had committed suicide? Soldiers were committing suicide every day, and it felt like the norm in some cases. Would I have to suck it up again, salute the flag and move on out? I was numb. I was distraught, lost, and confused. There were days when I didn't want to even get out of bed.

I couldn't afford to come undone I had 18 months left before I could retire, and I didn't want to get put out of the Army for not being able to do my job. I was responsible for putting together packages for the promotions of Generals. There was no margin of error. I couldn't afford to make any mistakes when it came to someone else's career, especially at this level. I was on autopilot get up, work, go home, repeat.

My mind kept wondering if I could have done something or said something that might have prevented Joe's suicide. I still asked God why. My head knew I wasn't responsible, but sometimes my heart still questions if I could have done something more.

My replacement hadn't shown up yet, so they asked me where to locate his insurance policies, notification documents, and personnel files. I knew all of Joe's information by heart. His ex-wife, his daughter, his insurance policies, everything. I was literally grieving in the casino, an hour away from home. But I was thankful for the hour drive home to collect my thoughts and concentrate, bring myself to level ground.

I wondered if anyone cared what I was going through. My friend had committed suicide. I was numb. This Soldier had been spiraling, and I felt as if no one did anything. Being a military intelligence Soldier, Joe didn't want to get help because it would likely have destroyed his career. But the signs were there.

I couldn't attend the funeral. I had just arrived at my new duty station. I was told by my boss to go home and get myself together. Mental health support for the grieving was nonexistent. My boss did apologize to me later on for not being supportive, and I accepted the apology. But, honestly, that was the norm. We dealt with our grief the best way we could. Alone. We were barely functioning at times noticeably and people would turn a blind eye and leave us to figure out our challenges on our own.

After this life curveball was hurled at me, I had to go deep into my closet and pray. I had prayed for everyone else, and now I had to pray for myself and ask where I was to go next. Finally, I decided to retire. After 20 years of Active Federal Service, I left the U.S. Army on January 31, 2013. I didn't have nor did I want a formal ceremony. I really just wanted to leave and put everything behind me, start a completely new life.

A year after I officially retired, my family did give me a formal retirement ceremony in North Carolina, and I loved it. My whole family got to attend. A retired First Sergeant came and "published" my retirement orders. Now it felt official.

Chapter 5

Finding my Way

I was happy when I retired. I was full of smiles. I had accomplished what I had set out to do. I had completed twenty years in the U.S. Army. I had kept my promise to my uncle. Despite my happiness, I realized when I retired, that time seemed to stand still. Nobody understood me; neither did I feel they understood what I had been through over the years. I felt like and still sometimes feel like an outsider trying to fit into a world not made for me.

In uniform, my mind automatically triggers to go somewhere else. I'm a Soldier. I have a creed to honor. I have an oath to live up to. I have a certain standard to represent. To us who wear the uniform, we understand what doesn't have to be stated verbally. When I pulled off my uniform for retirement, I was lost. *Did I really make the right decision?* It's not an easy task.

I had been in the Army all my adult life. The Army was full of structure. I had gotten my daily routine down to a science, and I knew almost everything I was going to do every day.

I wondered if retiring was the right move. *Lord, did I make the right decision?* I asked God repeatedly. I wondered if I had just been mad and in the heat of that anger and frustration just said, "I'm done." I cried out to God, "Lord, how do I go from combat boots to what people call normal?" I was not the same eighteen-year-old country girl that I was when I joined the military. My eyes had seen things I wished I had not seen. My ears had heard things not fit for anyone to hear. I, too, had said things that were not nice. How was I as a military woman going to move from combat to wholeness? I knew I had to keep moving, even through the moments of doubt, and questions of "what's next?" because tomorrow will be a different day, a new process. Someone who has never been in our shoes can't always relate. These were some of the questions I asked myself all the time.

Leaving the Army was a difficult decision to make. Actually, it was a total blur. I was still waking up early trying to figure out what to do with my life. It was so stressful even though I had no responsibilities to anyone but myself.

Many Soldiers are scared to make that leap so they stay in the military past the time they are supposed to stay. God may have said to stay a certain number of years and move on, but because the military seems to have life all laid out daily schedule, professional training and career advancement, clothing, exercise, next duty assignments sometimes it's hard to make that leap. Trust me, I know. We can feel invisible to the world outside of the military.

But being in the military was also very hard. Take female military personnel, for example. We wear so many hats that we hardly have any time for self-care. I had to do my job, of course, but I was often personal concierge to the families of fellow Soldiers. I was informally responsible for unit moral, anything that kept the office "happy." Women, being so few in number, are frequently assigned "gender-related" duties, particularly promotion ceremonies, farewell celebrations, birthday acknowledgements, baby showers and the like. I don't have any kids of my own and I only have one birthday a year like everyone else, but these responsibilities all fell to me because somehow as a woman, I was inherently an event planner.

Still, the whole time I was in the Army, I felt I was part of a cohesive team. No one could tell me I was not a part of the best Army in the world. I was a Soldier, not a woman. The Army told me I was first and foremost a Soldier, and I believed it to be true. I was a woman secondly, and mother/wife lastly.

For someone who has never been in the military, it may be hard to understand. Sometimes, a vivid dream the night before can influence the next day. Sometimes my bones hurt. Sometimes I just need a moment alone. Nothing is wrong, I just need a moment to collect myself. It's hard for civilians to understand why it takes veterans so long to assimilate back to the civilian life we started from. Some veterans don't ever assimilate at all; they live near a military base, work on a military base, and still think like Soldiers, Airmen, Sailors, or Marines.

All my adult life has been military structure, and literally, my life depended on it. I did my job with exceptional precision, because if I didn't, lives including my own would be in jeopardy.

I've always worked until the job was done, not up until it was my time to get off. It was very hard to assimilate into a civilian world with set hours because my whole life had been about working until the job was complete. Someone was depending on me having finished my job to completion in order to safely carry out the mission the next day.

I understood the lingo of my military family. "Hurry up and wait." "If you're five minutes early, you're late." Latrines not bathrooms. Chow at the dining hall not food at the cafeteria. The Post Exchange or PX not shopping area or the mall. We speak in acronyms and that's a comfort for me.

I've found that some civilians want me to "relax." I *am* relaxed *and* I'm doing my job. I don't want to let my standards down because I know first-hand what can happen when a person lets their standards down. Not being "on" in the moment is not an option. As a Soldier, I couldn't afford to perform or not perform based on emotion how I'm feeling today, who I like or don't like, who likes me or doesn't like me, what's going on at home and in my personal life. Emotional ties to performance would literally get me or someone in my battalion killed. It's hard to let that go.

When God told me to return to Madison, North Carolina after I retired, my whole world seemed to turn upside down. I wanted to retire near a military base. I wanted to stay around Soldiers. I wanted to be around those I felt understood me not walking around in a civilian setting feeling as though I didn't fit in. There I was, yet I felt invisible to the world and those around me. As big as the military is, it's small. We'll run into one another again maybe in the states, maybe on the other side of the world. Now that I'm retired, I truly miss the feeling of knowing I'll see people from my military family at my next duty station.

This new phase of my life felt awful. I felt like a misfit. I never was one to keep up with the styles, I wasn't into fashion, and that didn't bother me. But I still felt like I didn't fit in socially. My experiences weren't in sync with where everyone else was at this point in their lives. I was still looking at life through military eyes. How would I break that cycle? I knew I wasn't a misfit I had the awards, citations and commendations to prove it but I couldn't shake the feeling. It's not who I am, but in some ways it is who I am. I had to retrain my whole thought process.

I've had to just deal with it as best I could: PTSD, depression, anxiety, limiting physical conditions brought about from routine (though demanding) military activities, financial obligations to family that weren't anticipated, and living so far from a military installation (my comfort zone). I realize I've got to grasp the "nugget," the one piece of this life that I'm supposed to "get." This *reason*, this *season*, this *"why"* that I'm here. My latter shall be greater, and I believe that. I don't know the process, but I've got to walk it out. I'm not going to limit myself based on my own experiences. So many are suffering in silence. Well, I'm speaking up. I'll speak out for those without voices.

As veterans, we routinely experience people telling us how proud they are of us and how settling in will take time. Sometimes people have made insensitive comments like, "You're not in the military anymore, don't nobody want to hear talk like that." But how do we turn it off? Are we required to? We just can't turn off the way we were trained to think and behave all our adult lives. The way we walk, talk, reason, respond that's the way we were trained to be. It's not like there's a switch somewhere we can flip on and off to "act" like a civilian.

When I retired, I began to really think about how I could make myself turn off the recurring nightmares of war, and the nightmarish thoughts that flood my mind unexpectedly during the day. How do I turn off the haunting nightmares of my friend killing himself, and the feeling that somehow I knew he wasn't safe but was powerless to do anything but hope? How do I heal *me*?

I don't know why people say the things they say. I used to get mad, but I understand everyone has an opinion, it's what they think and feel based on their own environment. And I understand their right to freedom of speech is a freedom I vowed to protect, I literally fought to protect.

It takes a brave person to join an all-volunteer force like the Army and fight for the rights of others, even while surrendering many of our own rights. We're the brave ones. We took an oath to serve and protect and defend the red, white, and blue. We did it because we wanted to serve something bigger than ourselves. We are a collective family, a cohesive group. It's a selfless service, a leadership value. We should all hold our heads high, regardless of what anyone else says or thinks. I had to get over what other people said or thought.

I used to come home and cry because so many people didn't couldn't, wouldn't recognize the few of us who had raised our hands to keep this country safe for their freedoms. It was hurtful. But now I realize I'm the brave one, regardless of how ungrateful some people may feel towards my sacrifice.

Close friends and even some family members couldn't or didn't even try to begin to understand what I'd been through. They would look at me in horror and disbelief, and I'd shut down. So many people have told me what they couldn't do or what they wouldn't do, what they wouldn't put up with, and in saying so, fail to realize that they aren't respect the things I've actually done and had to put up with and suffered through and battled within myself for the greater good, for the higher call. They speak with such indifference and sometimes disdain. *Do they even realize?* We volunteered. We. Volunteered. I don't need accolades or praise, but respect is what I do expect. Respect is what I demand.

Chapter 6

God's Hand Directing My Steps

I tell people my retirement was straight from God. I truly sought God's hand and face before I requested to retire. God sent me these exact scriptures in answer:

> ²⁵ And I will restore to you the years that the locust hath eaten, the cankerworm, and the caterpillar, and the palmerworm, my great army which I sent among you.
>
> **Joel 2:25, KJV**

> ⁹The glory of this latter house shall be greater than of the former, saith the Lord of hosts: and in this place will I give peace, saith the Lord of hosts.
>
> **Haggai 2:9, KJV**

> ¹¹For I know the thoughts that I think toward you, saith the Lord, thoughts of peace, and not of evil, to give you an expected end.
>
> Jeremiah 29:11, KJV

I thought everything was going to be lined up and all would be well after God spoke these verses to me, especially restoration and thoughts of peace. Well, that was not even the case. Life threw me another curveball.

After I retired, I did all I could to avoid moving back to Madison, North Carolina. God insisted, "You will return home." I had to obey. So, I returned to Madison.

In Madison, finding a job was difficult. If I wasn't told I was overqualified for one job, I was told I was underqualified for another job. *Why won't they hire me?* I had served my country for 20 long years. I had a college degree that I earned while in the military. I had a good track record of longevity, reliability and dependability, and I knew I could learn on my feet. For goodness sake, I was a war veteran. (I say that with all humility. Sometimes as war veterans, we don't allow ourselves to be human because we have this superhuman title we believe we have to live up to.) I had actively served in war and I wore that as a badge of honor. To me, I had proven myself loyal, willing to lay down my life for what I believed. But being a war veteran was both an honor and a curse.

I learned from an employer that some employers were reluctant to hire veterans because they feared we might have flashbacks attributed to PTSD and hurt someone at work. We were considered a liability, a threat to the bottom line. There, another curveball was hurled right at me. Now I was being judged and discriminated against for serving my country! I have found this to be the story for so many veterans.

I was overqualified to be an administrative assistance. I was underqualified to be a Human Resources professional, although I had done the job for over fourteen years. Frustrated, I stopped looking for a job and went back to school.

I was minding my business. I was single with no real responsibility to anyone other than myself. I was a work-study student with the Vet Center in Greensboro. I was going to school at night with the money from the military G.I. Bill. I was studying business administration and social work, intending to be a peer specialist. Then, another curveball hit me. My niece was taken by the Department of Social Services and was about to be put into foster care. I could already see what was about to happen and how I would soon be involved.

We had a family meeting with my mother, my sisters, a caregiver, and other family members. I was reminded of a promise I made to my sister Karen in 2009 when I discovered she had terminal cancer; I told her I would make sure her granddaughter was taken care of. I assured her that her granddaughter as well as her nieces would be provided for. Immediately after my promise, my sister slipped into a coma.

Everyone came to the conclusion that I would be the best option to raise not just one, but two young children. Maybe it was my military training that allowed me to keep calm on the surface in the face of such enormous responsibility, but I was completely overw-helmed at the thought. My promise to my sister was more of a financial commitment and a promise to not let her grandchild end up in foster care. It wasn't my intention to raise someone else's child or children as my own, on my own.

In my mind, I cried, "Oh no, God, not me!" and God answered, "Why not you?" I began to list all the reasons I couldn't take in my nieces: my credit was messed up, I didn't have a full-time job, I never had kids and I didn't know how to be in charge of kids on a full-time basis. I gave a plethora of reasons, but God being omnipotent, omniscient God stayed silent because we both knew who was going to win that fight.

I didn't just take in one, but two of my nieces, who were aged 7 and 13. Taking in my nieces meant I would instantly become an Auntie-Mother (a name I gave myself as an aunt who stands in for a mother). This went against all I had planned for myself. I had promised God I was not going to be a single mother. Now, this curveball hit me and with it came two girls. I got in my bed and I cried for God to take it away.

Needless to say, God never gives us more than we can bear, and this responsibility was not taken away. The girls came to live with me and we started a new phase of our pilgrimage on this journey called Life.

Chapter 7

Recognizing My Weakness

The journey of life for me and the girls was rough. The girls didn't know me, and I, too, didn't know them well. Being stationed all over the world, I would drop into their lives during my "leave" (vacation time), and then leave back out again. We had no prior bonding time before we transitioned into a family of three. I know they thought I was crazy, and I for sure thought they were losing every piece of mind they had with the things they would say and do.

I was dealing with my many health issues, including my mental health. The girls, too, were dealing with their own issues. As a little, newly-formed family, we decided we needed to seek help from a professional therapist. I must say, the therapist was and continues to be God sent.

I now know that a therapist doesn't hold bias against anyone in your family, regardless of what is said. More importantly, they have no bias against *you* and they are there to help *you*. It was something I had to learn as I walked this walk from "combat to wholeness." While in the military, seeing a therapist was considered almost a career-ending experience. As a veteran outside of the Army, I had to train my mind that it's time to take care of me Katina, the woman and not the combat Soldier. Today, I have to make myself take a leave day if I need to. I have to understand that the earth will continue to spin if I take lunch or get my hair done. I'm a work in progress.

At the Vet Clinic, I was assigned to a therapist to help me walk out my issues of guilt, anxiety, doubt, low self-esteem, and learning to love myself. I believe it is hard to love others when you can't look yourself in the mirror and love yourself.

I knew deep within my heart that I had done all the Army had asked of me to do. Yet I wondered how I was to adjust from the Army life to this crazy civilian world. How did I stop feeling invisible and putting on a fake smile when deep down I was hurting and didn't want to get out of bed? How was I supposed to help my nieces find their way when all they wanted was for their own mother and father to love them?

My therapist would let me cry without saying a thing. She would not judge me. She wouldn't tell me how to act or how to feel or what was normal. She would just sit there and let me cry. We finally got around to talking about how I often would wake up in the middle of the night believing something was perilously wrong, that I was in physical danger. On the nights when this happened, I'd have to verbally tell myself, "I'm okay, I'm fine." I would then go and check on the girls and find them sound asleep. But the pattern of interrupted sleep and the adrenaline rush and the mental fragility in those moments left me physically exhausted and began to take its toll.

But there was something else I had kept bottled up inside and had to release before its pressure took an even greater toll on me than the nightmares.

I was finally able to talk to my therapist about my friend who had committed suicide. That was such a bitter pill to swallow because he pinky-promised me he would be just fine. We had picked out his retirement land, and we both were excited, believing he was ready for the next phase of his life. And then it was all gone.

Sometimes I still get overwhelmed with guilt. I still ask myself what I could have done to prevent his suicide. I miss my friend.

"I can't tell you when this pain will heal," my therapist told me one day at one of our sessions, "or when you may be able to move beyond it. Healing is a process." She was right; it's a process. Things could go well one minute, but within seconds something can be said or done that could throw me right back into absolute despair. What do we do? We were trained to handle combat in the moment, but we were not trained to be healed afterwards. I started walking out my healing with counseling and therapy. It's still a daily process. I have to remind myself that I am not invisible and people do see my pain but they may not know what to say or how to help me overcome my pain.

As for my girls dealing with their own struggles, they each had their own therapist and they have come a long way. The oldest has her journal and continues to journal her thoughts and feelings, taking it day by day. When she was finally leaving for college, I reminded her she didn't have any expectations to live up to. I cautioned her to stay focused on positive things and continue writing in her journal. My youngest niece remains in therapy, and knowing how it has benefitted me, I fully support her.

(Parents, it's okay more than okay for your child to see a therapist. It doesn't mean you have done anything wrong or you are bad at parenting. It's just that sometimes your child may feel more comfortable speaking with a stranger that will not be biased. You may not intentionally be biased, but you are their parent, and they are your child. They may seek objective views that we, as parents, can't always provide. Just think about that.)

We are not dealing with kids from twenty or thirty years ago from back in my day where what the parent and child experienced was common. We are dealing with social media, peer pressure where the stakes are so much higher, and all manner of other issues that are trying to still and kill our children. God said:

> **³ Lo, children are a heritage of the LORD: and the fruit of the womb is his reward.**
>
> **Psalm 127:3, KJV**

No matter how we may think sometimes or feel like our children are behaving as if they are the "spawn of the devil," we have to remember they assuredly are not and we should not allow the devil to have them. I declared that the devil will not have my nieces and I will not give up.

Sometimes they fight me and we fight each other. We've all been through a lot and in different ways, and we weren't there to witness each other's past pain. In spite of all this, God has a great work set out for them and me. To be honest, I've wanted to give up and throw in the towel several times. God, however, kept reminding me that he has me in the palm of his hand.

Children will do and say what they see us do or say. We have to speak positive words to our children. Always speak life. I always speak life over my nieces. I have tried my best to keep my nieces in church and get them active in positive activities. On the days I want to throw in the towel, God throws it right back and says, "Pick it up and wipe your tears and move forward." He's brought me this far through some of the worst challenges I could have ever imagined for my own life. Quite possibly, it was so I could be here with unrestrained empathy as my nieces successfully navigate their own battlefield experiences.

Chapter 8

Loving Ourselves

I'll share what I have learned after all my years of service to the military: Women, we have to learn to love ourselves. We always tend to want to put others before ourselves. As an Army Soldier and a leader, that was my job taking care of Soldiers. Once that was gone, I felt like I was useless and invisible to the world. I often asked myself, "Who am I? What am I to do with my life now?" It was hard for me to look in the mirror and say, "I am beautiful and I love me!" We want to deal with our flaws and weaknesses piece by piece instead of looking at the totality of who we are.

We identify and label our weaknesses, recognizing them real or imagined one by one. But rather than separating ourselves into deficiencies, we have to start putting ourselves back together, building ourselves up into who we were created to be.

No, letting go of our own hurt and pain, and forgiving ourselves and those who have hurt us is not easy. But it is *necessary* to our healing process. We are consistently being labeled and accepting an identity as the "strong ones." We are depended upon and feel a responsibility to keep the family together but who is keeping us together?

Women, especially combat veterans, shut ourselves off and push our own selves aside for the comfort of others. We "suck it up and move on" to make everyone else feel okay. I had to take time to breathe and know that in addition to being a woman not the eternal Soldier I thought myself to be I am human, I am valued and I am loved. I have to take care of myself.

There are so many things I've had to learn and now I am desperate to share with others who have been in my situation, whether surviving combat, financial stress, unemployment, loss of a friend or family member, single parenthood, unanticipated responsibility, or just overwhelmed with life. When we think nobody else cares about us, know that God cares. When we are about to make a permanent solution to a temporary problem, know that tomorrow is a new day to start over. We all have changed and we will forever change, but God has promised to remain the same; he loved us from the very beginning and that won't change.

> ⁴ Long before he laid down earth's foundations, he had us in mind, had settled on us as the focus of his love, to be made whole and holy by his love.
>
> Ephesians 1:4, MSG

We have to recognize our weaknesses and love every one of our flaws. We have to stop beating ourselves up and know that it's alright to seek help, to have that one great friend who will just sit and talk with us and walk us through our darkest moments without being judgmental. As my therapist said, it's a process, but it is one that can be won. I have a saying that I say to myself: "One second, one moment and one day at a time equals winning!" Stay the course and understand there are plans, purpose, and destiny for your life.

Chapter 9

Purpose, Plan and Process to Wholeness

My journey along this path of life has had its twists and turns, ups and downs. I never thought I would be a Combat Veteran Soldier. Neither did I ever envision being an Auntie-Mother. My idea of an ideal life for me? I was to be married to the love of my life and live with him in that home I mentioned earlier with that white picket fence. I also dreamt of having two children and living very comfortably. That was my ideal life, but that was not God's plan for me. It's funny how we try to tell God what we want in life as though we know everything. As the saying goes: "If you want to make God laugh, tell Him your plans."

I continue to seek God's face about my healing and wholeness and where I am supposed to be in my life. I had to surrender and let God move in my life. I couldn't heal myself and nobody else could heal me. Only God could heal me in the true way I needed healing and restoration. Yes, God has given the doctors all the tools to use to help in the healing process, but only God can bring true healing. And sometimes healing only comes with time.

Becoming a Soldier was not instantaneous. I didn't become a Soldier overnight. In the same way I gradually became a Soldier and refined myself as a Soldier over time, adjusting to life after retirement takes time. I could not instantly turn off the way I had been trained to think, act, and be for over twenty years. I realized I may have had very unrealistic expectations of my transition, thinking the transition was going to be easy, second nature. God never said it would be. But he did promise to strengthen me, and help me, and keep me upright when I felt like falling, never to stand again. He said:

> ¹⁰ **Fear thou not; for I am with thee: be not dismayed; for I am thy God: I will strengthen thee; yea, I will help thee; yea, I will uphold thee with the right hand of my righteousness.**
>
> **Isaiah 41: 10, KJV**

I just had to learn to trust the process.

As a female veteran, my heart goes out to other female veterans. We are unique in all our ways. We have played multiple roles such as being Soldiers, Airman, Sailor, Marine, mother, friend, counselor, and many other roles while in uniform. Now we have to learn to love and take care of ourselves. That can be such a hard thing for us to do, to even ask of ourselves, but it must be done. As women veterans, we now have to learn how to put the combat boots away and walk into our wholeness.

As a female veteran, I took pride in being a "Super Trooper," being rough and tough. I enjoyed that I was looked at as just another Soldier, not for my gender as a woman Soldier. I can't speak for all female veterans I am speaking from my experience only. But I wanted to yell loud like the guys, drink like the guys, and curse like the guys. I took pride in all of that.

After leaving the Army, I was no longer a Soldier. I had to become a lady. I had to conduct myself as such. I had never been one to wear dresses, tight-fitting clothes, high-heel shoes or things of that nature. I had to be taught all of that. This may sound crazy to some people, but it's true. I truly *enjoyed* my ruggedness while in the Army. Don't get me wrong, as I got older, some changes were easier to make than others. But some other things took time. And there are still some changes I'm still working on making to this day.

Over the last couple of years, I've come a long way from a being combat veteran and I'm working my way to wholeness. I've learned to live to please God. I've taken time to meditate and understand my purpose in life. I've found my purpose to be an encouragement to those who feel as though the world has dropped everything on their shoulders, and to be a comfort to those who are dealing with the same feelings I had of being invisible. I believe I am to be a source of strength to those who feel as though they are walking through life alone. My purpose is to help female veterans like me, who might be suffering from PTSD, anxiety, and depression.

Many times, we as women suffer in silence because we don't want to be labeled. We don't want to be seen as different. We don't want to be looked down upon as though we are one of the deadly plagues. We don't want to be a stereotype. So many women suffer in silence, feeling as if they are invisible to the entire world. Sometimes it feels as though we are physically there, but we can be so broken down and downtrodden that we can't even lift our heads, not to mention the ever-present internal turmoil. Well, tie a knot in your rope and hold on. You're not alone, and you don't have to go through those feelings alone. God says in his Word:

> 18 If your heart is broken, you'll find God right there; if you're kicked in the gut, he'll help you catch your breath.
>
> Psalm 34:18, MSG

Many people have no passion, purpose, or plan for their lives, not because they don't want it or don't seek it, they just don't know how to find it. After being in the military for so many years where you instinctively know your purpose and plan, and often find your passion, it's hard to transition and discover it all over again in something completely different. We can find ourselves stuck in dead-end jobs, simply existing without fulfillment.

Discovering our purpose helps us to avoid living a life without passion. Once we find our purpose, we have to tap into it and really work it. It was once said to me, "We don't work to live, we live to work." That means if we are not passionate about what we are doing in our lives, we're just there for the paycheck. Such a life means we're not truly living because we're not imparting into other people's lives and we're missing out on the passion, purpose, and plan for life.

My advice is to take a step away from naysayers and surround yourself with positive people. Surround yourself with people that will tell you the truth about yourself. Naysayers will suck the life out of you and if you don't take heed, you will be living your life for them and in the way they determine. Surround yourself with positive people that will tell you the truth to your face even when you don't want to hear it and encourage you to pick yourself up, dust yourself off, and move forward. Move with people that encourage you to be a better person. You don't have to be the smartest or the most skilled. It just takes time, and the great thing is that we all have time. Whether it feels like it or not, we do.

> 11 I returned and saw under the sun, that the race is not to the swift, nor the battle to the strong, neither yet bread to the wise, nor yet riches to men of understanding, nor yet favor to men of skill; but time and chance happeneth to them all.
>
> Ecclesiastes 9:11, KJV

My walk from being a combat veteran to wholeness continues daily. It is an ongoing process. It has not been easy, there are still some days I don't want to get up and face the day. However, on such days when I pray, God reminds me not to give up or quit. He reminds me that healing is a process that must be walked out. I believe God gave me my nieces so that we could save each other's lives.

In your daily life, always remember to PUSH Pray Until Something Happens. We should know that our work is not in vain.

> ³ Knowing this, that the trying of your faith worketh patience.
>
> ⁴ But let patience have her perfect work, that ye may be perfect and entire, wanting nothing.
>
> James 1: 3, 4, KJV

Life will throw us curveballs once in a while sometimes very often and very quickly. I won't lie, sometimes these curveballs will hit hard, but we all must stay on course and finish our race. As long as we remain on the path that God specifically designed for us and trust God's process, we will win. The people who are attached to us will come to trust God, too, and in the end, we all will win.

Life is a journey, and it's not completed overnight. It's a process that goes on every day. We must wake up every day and decide what type of day we will have. This life isn't easy and we didn't ask for the hardships we endure. But it's what we make of this life that determines what we will get out of it. Sometimes all we can do is put one foot in front of the other. Guess what? That's perfectly fine. We just have to keep moving.

I am learning that I can't live my live for any other human being but Katina. And *you* can't live for anyone but *yourself*. Once we start to remove the baggage in our lives that's weighing us down and holding us back, then we can start to truly breathe.

And it's okay to say "no." We need to stop allowing other people's pain to become our pain, and embracing it with our verbal or implied "yes." We have to learn to say "No!" and be completely okay with honoring ourselves, our time, our boundaries. We have to say it in such a way that when we say "no," it is final and there is no discussion about it, not because we are unreasonable, but because we are grown adults capable of knowing what it is we want to do and don't want to do without coercion or guilt.

As I write this, I am still learning to deal with the word "no." Once we get to the point where we love ourselves more than we fear offending or pleasing others, it will be easier to say, "no." The freedom that comes with it is immeasurable. I am not completely at that point yet, but I am a lot closer than I was before.

The quest is to keep making progress in the healing process and to continue moving forward. It doesn't matter how small the progress is that we make, all that matters is that we are making progress. Taking our time to find our purpose, planning, and walking in our healing and wholeness belongs solely to us.

Let's not put ourselves in a box made by other people: height, weight, hair, how we are supposed to think and behave. These boxes can be very contradictory and leave us feeling lost and confused. Let's find our purpose, map our plans, and walk in our own healing and wholeness. We shall live and not die because we have the victory!

ABOUT THE AUTHORS

Katina Patterson was an 18-year-old Private when she found herself in Kuwait supporting Desert Storm. Surviving the ground war, she went on to serve 20 years in the Army only to discover Army life was the only life she knew transition back to civilian life was inconceivably difficult. *But God.* Katina shares her struggle towards finding wholeness after combat as an opportunity to encourage fellow veterans who suffer from Post-Traumatic Stress Disorder, depression and anxiety as a result of their dedication and honorable service to this nation.

Tracey Nicole Hayes was a 20-year-old midshipman studying at the U.S. Naval Academy during Desert Storm. After 24 years in the Navy, she retired as a Human Resources Officer and followed her passion for writing into a second career. As fate would have it, she and Katina met at an event honoring women veterans where they were both guest speakers. In this resulting collaboration with Katina, she acknowledges the women who have sacrificially paved the way so that others can fulfill their dreams of serving in the U.S. Armed Forces without limitations.

Made in the USA
Monee, IL
14 March 2021